The Complete Kids' Guide

"let's go!"

"Marvelous!"

Solar Eclipse

"Wonderful!"

"Awesome!"

the
GREAT AMERICAN

SOLAR ECLIPSE

of

August

21st

2017

"WOW!"

"AMAZING!"

"Beautiful!"

and Activity Book

Hi! My name is ECLIPSO, and I'll be your guide. My sunglasses are awesome, right? They are official, solar eclipse approved viewing glasses!

this book belongs to:

_____

If you don't have your official, eclipse approved viewing glasses yet, be sure to get them. Regular sunglasses will NOT work! DO NOT look at the sun with regular sunglasses

contact storiesinscience@gmail.com to request information

TABLE of CONTENTS

Eclipse Begins!

Partial Phases
*During the partial phase of the eclipse, part of the sun is still visible. Only look at the partial eclipse through your solar—viewing glasses.

TOTALITY!

TOTALITY!
*During totality, the moon completely covers the sun. If you are lucky enough to see totality, ask a grown up when it is okay to remove your viewing glasses during totality.

Eclipse Ends

What's the Big Deal?

SCIENCE GUIDE

to the

GREAT AMERICAN SOLAR ECLIPSE

of 2017

What is a SO

 "in only 70 words!"

The **MOON** goes around the **EARTH**.

The **EARTH** goes around the **SUN**.

The **SUN** is very big and far away.

YOU!

The **MOON** is much smaller but closer.

So from **EARTH**, the **SUN** and **MOON** look the same size.

As the **EARTH** spins, the **SUN** and **MOON** look like they are moving across the sky.

And sometimes the **MOON** passes right in front of the **SUN**.

This is a **SOLAR ECLIPSE!**

"Hey, that's me!"

And the Great American Solar Eclipse of 2017 is extra special because...

Why is this

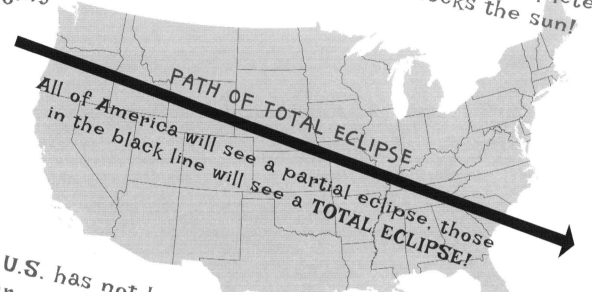

The TOTAL eclipse will be visible only in the United States!

A total eclipse is when the moon completely blocks the sun!

PATH OF TOTAL ECLIPSE

All of America will see a partial eclipse, those in the black line will see a TOTAL ECLIPSE!

The U.S. has not had a total solar eclipse in 26 years! And that was only in Hawaii.

TOTAL solar eclipses are TOTALLY AMAZING!

ECLIPSE HISTORY!

"This one's going down in eclip-story!"

* Eclipses occur all over the world, and have been written about for over 2500 years.
* Before scientists explained solar eclipses, people thought they were omens or messages from the gods.
* The next total eclipse to pass across the U.S. will be on April 8th, 2024. This will also be a very exciting eclipse!
* The first photograph of a total eclipse was on July 28th, 1851.

one Special?

"Hey, I'm ALWAYS special!"

The Sun's atmosphere is called the CORONA. You can only see it during TOTALITY.

The corona is millions of degrees. That's HOT!

FUN SUN FACTS!

* the **SUN** is 93 million miles away!
* the **SUN** burns a gas called hydrogen. This burning makes helium – the same stuff in balloons.
* the **SUN** is over 4.5 **BILLION** years old, and still has 4.5 billion years to go!
* light from the **SUN** takes about 8 minutes to reach Earth!

ENOUGH MOON STUFF!

* the **MOON** is about 1/4 the size of Earth.
* if you weighed 100 pounds on Earth, you would only weigh about 16 pounds on the **MOON!**
* the **MOON** is only 230,000 miles away. That's a lot less than 93 million!
* the **MOON** is covered in a fine dust called 'regolith'.

"Some people say a total eclipse looks like a black hole in the sky."

"Sometimes crickets chirp during TOTALITY because the crickets think it is night time. Silly crickets!"

OFFICIAL NASA
MAP ON THE NEXT PAGE!

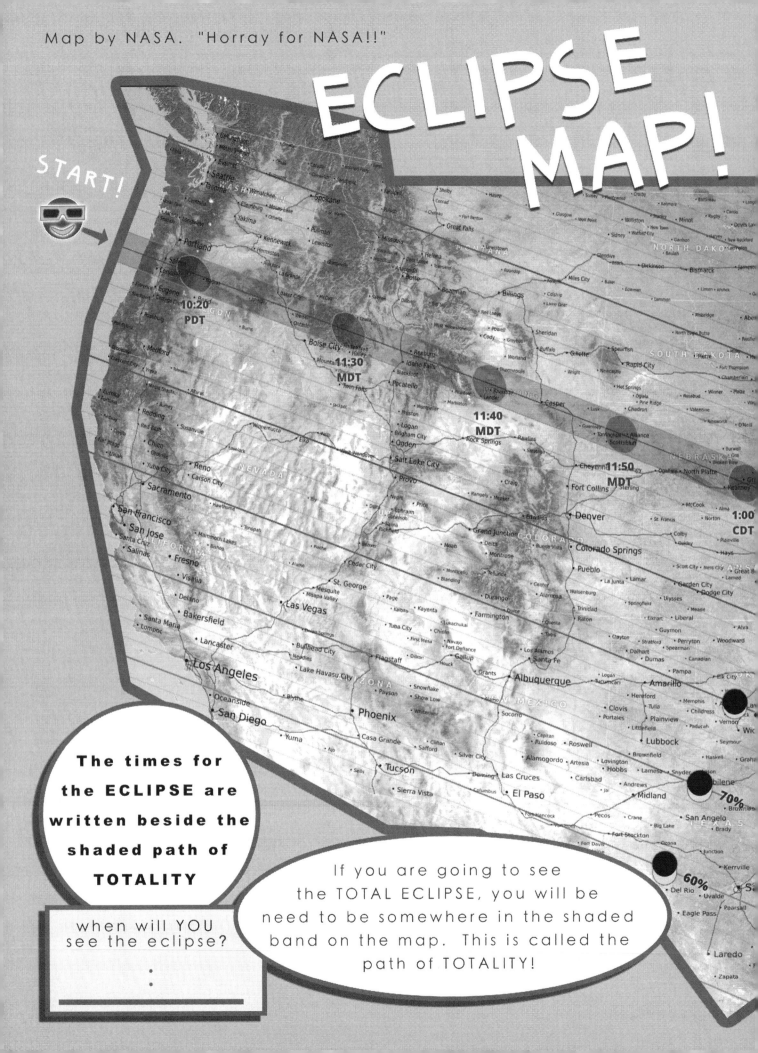

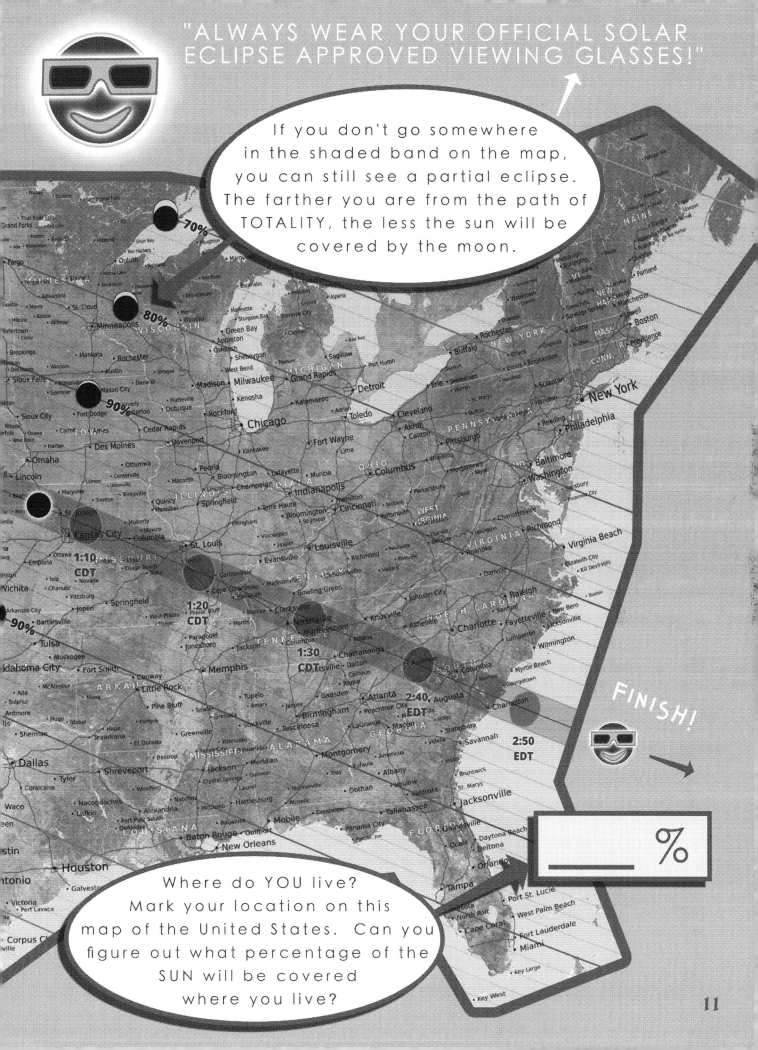

What Should I Bring?

ESSENTIAL ITEMS and CHECKLIST

for the BEST ECLIPSE ADVENTURE EVER!

☐ YOUR OFFICIAL SOLAR ECLIPSE APPROVED VIEWING GLASSES!!!!!!

☐ Sunscreen and water! While you're waiting for the eclipse, you might get thirsty, and hopefully the sky will be cloud-free!

☐ THIS BOOK! and a pencil.

☐ Lunch! The eclipse will take place around lunchtime for much of the country. Pack a lunch so you don't have to worry about missing the big event.

☐ Something to look forward to in case the sky is cloudy and you can't see the eclipse. That way, if you don't see it, you'll be less dissapointed. I plan on getting ice cream if clouds ruin the day!

Play these ECLIPSE activities for lots of FUN, FUN, FUN!

"Let's Play!"

Fun STUFF!

"are you ready?"

ACTIVITIES, GAMES, PUZZLES, and MORE!

"Some games are easy, some are hard. Try them all!"

"more is good!"

"I like more."

Find answers in the back.

"nice shades!"

DESIGN your own ECLIPSE-APPROVED viewing glasses!

Your official, solar eclipse viewing glasses might look something like this.
Cover these pictures with your awesome designs! And color them too!

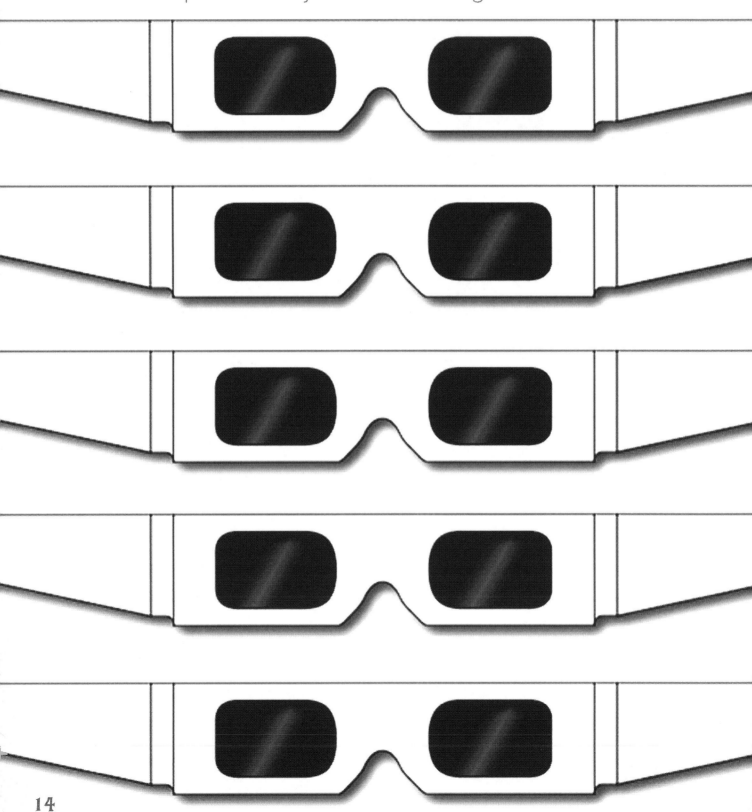

```
e s p i l c e e e c
c c l i s c c s s e
l s l i l i l p p e
i e e i c l i i i e
p l p i p s p l l p
s s s c l s s c c e
e c l i p s e e e l
e c l i p s e l c i
e s p i l c e e p e
s e e s p s p e e c
```

HOW FAST CAN YOU FIND THE WORD "eclipse" 10 TIMES?

Can you do it in under 2 minutes?   Time yourself!

15

SUPER-DUPER STATE SHAPES

The path of TOTALITY goes through these 12 states. Can you match the shape of each state with its name? You can check your answers on the map on the next page.

Idaho

Nebraska

Missouri

Kentucky

Wyoming

Illinois

North Carolina

Oregon

Kansas

Tennessee

Georgia

South Carolina

Why did the moon pass in front of the sun?

To get to the other side!

How many states do you know?

Label as many states as you can on this map of the U.S.
If you can get all 48, you're a state expert!

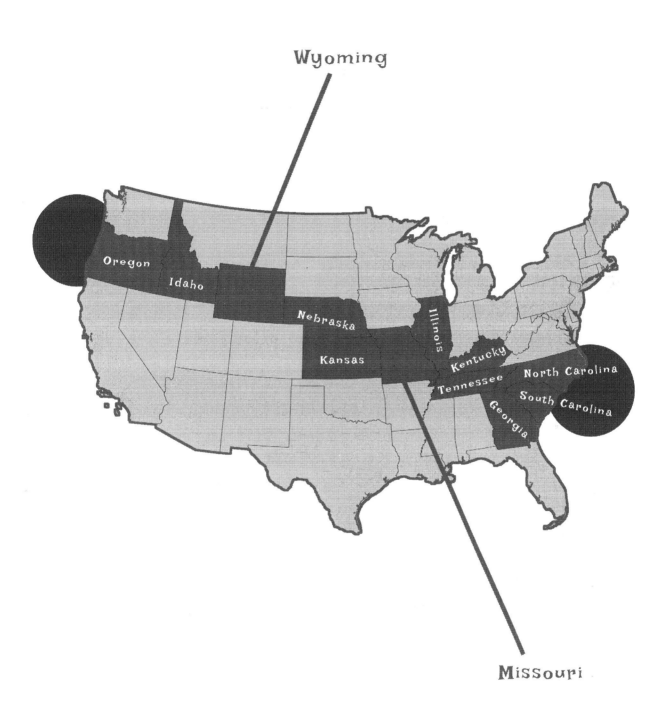

"HELP! Someone turned me into dots and stuck me next to this maze!"

"Can you redraw me and help me find my way out?"

18

the PLANETS

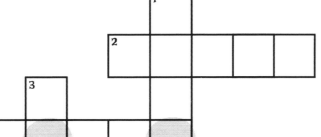
Complete the crossword puzzle.

The letters in the gray circles can be unjumbled to make a new word.

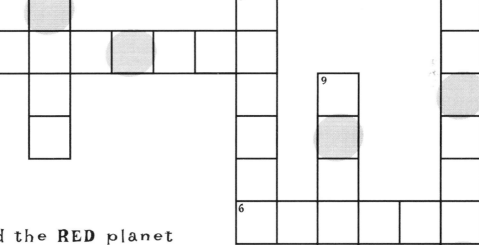

1. also called the **RED** planet
2. the planet we call home
3. the planet closest to the sun
4. also called "the morning or evening star"
5. has a big red "EYE"
6. the one with the largest ring
7. the big blue gas planet
8. **SUNARU** spelled backwards
9. it used to be called a planet, but not anymore

Unjumble the letters to find the secret word!

"I'm not little, if the EARTH was as big as this dot .
the SUN would be as big as a basketball!"

```
N  N  N  N  N
N  U  U  U  N
N  U  S  U  N
N  U  U  U  N
N  N  N  N  N
```

How many times can you find the word SUN?

(frontwards, backwards, upside down, and diagonal)

your answer:

SUN WORDSEARCH

```
S S S S S S S S S
S U U U U U U U S
S U N N N N N U S
S U N U U U N U S
S U N U S U N U S
S U N U U U N U S
S U N N N N N U S
S U U U U U U U S
S S S S S S S S S
```

How many times can you find the word SUN?

your answer: [ ]

 FLAGS!

MANY FLAGS HAVE SYMBOLS OF THE SUN, MOON, AND STARS. HERE ARE 8 EXAMPLES IN BLACK & WHITE. WHAT COLORS DO YOU THINK THESE FLAGS ARE IN REAL LIFE? COLOR THEM, AND THEN LOOK THEM UP TO SEE IF YOU WERE CLOSE!

South Carolina

Texas

Pakistan

Alaska

Bangladesh

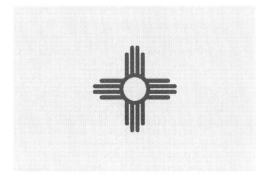

New Mexico

Namibia

Uruguay

F L A G S !

DESIGN YOUR OWN FLAGS WITH SYMBOLS OF THE SUN, THE MOON, AND STARS!

"NICE FLAGS!"

Sunny words
WORDSEARCH

```
m a e b r i g h t
g e z a l b a p n
l l s r u l i i a
i i o h m n g e i
g l o w i n g r d
h i s u n n y c a
t h u o o l e i r
e r i f u s r n n
l f i a s f h g m
```

Can you find these 12 sunny words?

bright
luminous
shine
glowing

fire
glow
light
sunny

piercing
ablaze
radiant
beam

24

Dark Words
WORDSEARCH

```
l g k y a e h i u
t y o r m d b i d
n l b a a o l a r
i g s h a d o w y
a k c a l b c l y
f d u s k y k d g
i k r i r n e b n
d o e s h a d y i
t h g i n l m i d
```

Can you find these 12 dark words?

dusky

shadowy

shady

faint

dark

gloomy

black

dim

blocked

obscure

night

dingy

25

MOON
wordsearch

```
M O M O O N
O O N M O M
N N O N N O
M O O N O O
N O M O O N
M N O O M O
```

How many times can you find the word MOON?

hint: there's more than 10

your answer _____

MOON CITY!

draw an awesome moon city

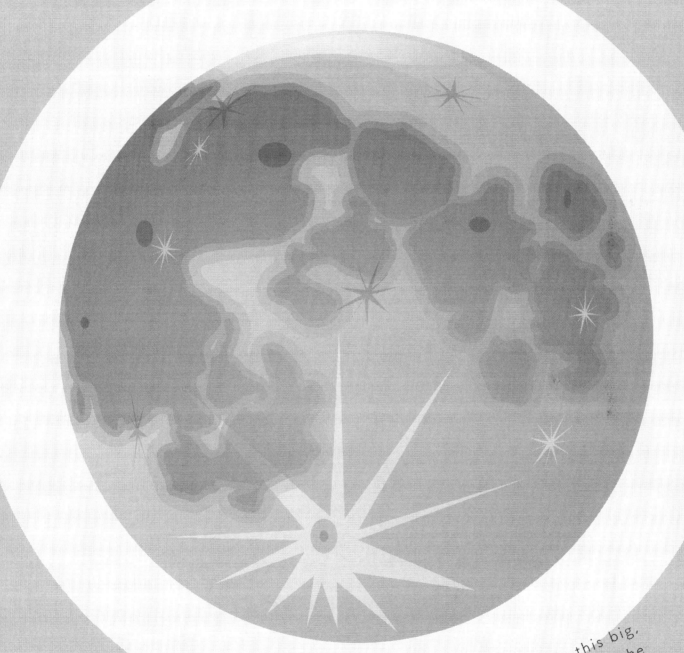

"Where's the cheese factory?"

"If the MOON were only this big, the SUN would be about half the size of a football field! and EARTH would be about two feet wide"

the "Where Would You Live?" Quiz

What if you figured out how to build cities on the Sun and the Moon. WOW!
Now you can move there! Circle your answers to the questions below to find
out if you would rather move to the Moon, the Sun, or stay on Earth.

Would you rather...
A. stay up late and sleep-in the next morning
B. go to bed early and wake up early
C. go to bed and wake up at a normal time

What bird do you like the most...
A. owl
B. robin
C. chicken

Would you rather...
A. live on the ocean
B. live in a desert
C. live on a farm

If you could be a mythical creature, would you be...
A. a mermaid
B. a dragon
C. a bigfoot

What color do you like the most...
A. blue
B. red
C. green

Would you rather eat...

A. pumpkin pie

B. strawberry lemonade

C. baked potatoes

What bug do you like the most...

A. dragonfly

B. ladybug

C. ant

Do you prefer...

A. rocks

B. fire

C. grass

"THIS QUIZ IS SILLY"

IF YOU ANSWERED...

Mostly **A**'s : Pack your bags, you're going to the **MOON**! Blue dragonflys will serve you pumpkin pie all night, and you won't have to go to bed early.

Mostly **B**'s : Get your sunscreen, because you're going to live on the **SUN**. It's gonna be hot, but you'll be able to drink strawberry lemonade with friendly sun-dragons all day long!

Mostly **C**'s : There's no need for you to do anything, you're an **EARTH** dweller. You can stay right here and grow potatoes on your farm!

ON THE MOON Mad Lib

DIRECTIONS

Fill in the blanks of the mad lib WITHOUT reading the story first, or ask someone to help you. When you fill in all the blanks, read your mad lib out loud, LAUGH, and then draw a picture of your silly scene!

If I lived on the moon, I would bring my best friend _____.   We would build

_____s and play _____ and eat
_____ type of building _____ _____ game or sport

_____ all day. Our moon boots would look
_____ food

like giant _____ feet, and we would
_____ animal

have pets that had the body of a _____
_____ animal

and the head of a _____. We would wear
_____ animal

_____ during the day because it would
_____ winter clothing

be so hot, and _____ at night because it
_____ summer clothing

would be so cold.

"That's MAD!"

Draw a picture of your life on the moon!:

30

How many smaller words can you make out of the letters in the word "eclipse"? Add up your score below, then check the back of the book for answers!

"Shouldn't that be an O?"

eclipse

3 letter words	4 letter words	5 letter words	6 letter words
LIP			
1 point each	2 points each	3 points each	6 points each

TOTAL POINTS = _____

SUN SYMBOLS

People have been
drawing pictures of
the sun for thousands of years.
Here are some examples of suns
with faces. Color them or give them
sunglasses!

"This one looks familiar. Can you find it somewhere else in this book?"

DESIGN YOUR OWN
SUN SYMBOLS

use the circles below to design
your own sun symbols!

"no one has shades like ME!"

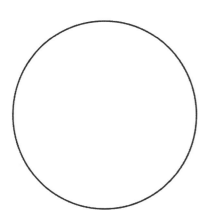

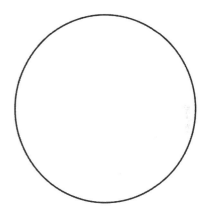

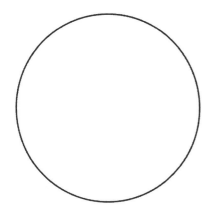

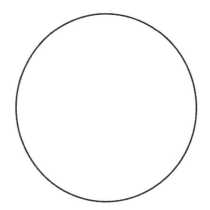

the planets

can you find the names of all 8 planets in this wordsearch?

```
S E U S M U S E
U Y T A T U E E
N U R T S E N R
A S N U A E U E
R T N R C A T T
U E U N U R P N
V J U P I T E R
U U E R E H N M
```

MERCURY **JUPITER**

VENUS **SATURN**

EARTH **URANUS**

MARS **NEPTUNE**

ECLIPSE STORY STARTERS!

Use these story starters to tell hilarious eclipse stories.
Find another person to take turns adding to the story.
Keep going as long as you can!

 "I love stories about me, they're TOTALL-IT-Y awesome"

1. Once upon a time, some kids went to see the eclipse, but when it happened, the **SUN** fell from the sky and...

2. It was a dark and stormy night – the night before a total solar eclipse. We heard a noise! It sounded like...

3. On our way to the solar eclipse, we took a wrong turn. We drove for hours and ended up driving all the way to...

4. Three days after the solar eclipse, something very strange happened. We all felt – unusual. And then we all turned into...

5. During the total solar eclipse of **2017**, it stuck that way! The **MOON** didn't keep crossing the **SUN**. It looked like a black hole in the sky for weeks! And then, something came out of it...

Eclipse Day!
WHAT TO EXPECT on AUGUST 21st

Viewing Guide for the Big Day

1. Eclipse Day will be very exciting! Get to where you will be viewing the eclipse early. There could be heavy traffic – lots of people will want to see this eclipse.

2. When the partial eclipse begins, everyone will be excited! There might be shouting and cheering! For about an hour, the moon will slowly move in front of the sun. The absolute most important thing to do is to wear your official, eclipse-approved viewing glasses at all times when viewing the partial eclipse. **NEVER EVER** look at the sun without your eclipse glasses!

3. **TOTALITY!** If you are in the path of totality, you will experience a **TOTAL ECLIPSE** and the moon will completely block the sun! This will last a minute or two depending on where you are. It's **AWESOME!** It will get dark and cold and feel like sunset. You might see stars. Follow a grown-ups instructions on whether you can remove your glasses during totality.

4. When totality ends, you will be very excited about what you just saw. Celebrate with your friends and family! Jump up and down! If you didn't see totality, you can still jump up and down!

5. Unfortunately, sometimes clouds block the eclipse. If this happens to you, it will be sad and dissapointing. Everyone around you will be glum. But hopefully, you prepared something to look forward to if this does happen. Now is the time for that thing!

6. After the eclipse, draw a picture of your experience and write a story about it on the following pages. Remember this exciting adventure forever!

My Eclipse Drawing

When the eclipse is over, draw what it looked like, and draw everyone that shared the amazing experience with you.

After the Eclipse
WRITE your ECLIPSE STORY!

Did you have fun? Did you see the eclipse?

I hope you did! Now, write all about your adventure so you'll never forget. From getting ready to going home, tell **YOUR** eclipse story...

_____

_____

_____

_____

_____

_____

_____

_____

_____

_____

_____

ANSWERS:

page 20 - the word "sun" is spelled 8 times

page 21 - the word "sun" is spelled 64 times

page 26 - the word "moon" is spelled 11 times

page 19 - the unjumbled words spell "eclipse"

1. mars
2. earth
3. mercury
4. venus
5. jupiter
6. saturn
7. neptune
8. uranus
9. pluto

page 31 - these are the most common words that come from letters in "eclipse":

3 letter words: lip, eel, sip, see, lie, pie, ice
4 letter words: lips, eels, clip, lies, slip, pile, pies, peel
5 letter words: piece, piles, sleep, peels, clips, slice, spice
6 letter words: pieces, splice

"If you can't find a word in a crossword puzzle, keep looking - they are all there somewhere. Look up, down, backwards, across, and diagonally."

Want to Know More About Eclipses?

Check out these eclipse websites. YES!

www.eclipse2017.org

eclipse2017.nasa.gov

!!!!! ECLIPSE VIEWING SAFETY and DISCLAIMER !!!!!

Viewing a solar eclipse is safe if done properly. Follow all instructions on your solar eclipse approved viewing glasses. The author of **SOLAR ECLIPSE 2017** is not liable for any improper viewing of the eclipse. If you do not have solar eclipse approved viewing glasses, **DO NOT** look at the sun. For a more detailed guide to viewing the eclipse safely, visit this page:

eclipse2017.nasa.gov/safety

Made in the USA
San Bernardino, CA
13 August 2017